BEN ELLIS is a Gippsland-born playwright and columnist, whose previous plays include *Eclipses, Select Committee for Imagining a Certain Maritime Incident, 360 Positions in a One Night Stand* (co-writer), *Loading Zone, Outpatients, Post Felicity* (winner of the 2001 Malcolm Robertson Prize), *Falling Petals* (winner of the 2003 Australian National Playwrights' Centre / New Dramatists Award, and shortlisted for a 2004 NSW Premier's Literary Play Award), *These People* (shortlisted for the 2004 NSW Premier's Literary Award: Community Relations Commission Award) and an adaptation of Franz Kafka's *The Metamorphosis*.

ALSO BY BEN ELLIS

Post-Felicity
These People

Falling Petals

BEN ELLIS

CURRENCY PRESS
The performing arts publisher

CURRENCY PLAYS

First published in 2003
by Currency Press Pty Ltd,
PO Box 2287, Strawberry Hills NSW 2012 Australia
enquiries@currency.com.au
www.currency.com.au

in association with Playbox Theatre, Melbourne

This revised edition published 2006

Reprinted 2009, 2012, 2013, 2015, 2021, 2022

NATIONAL LIBRARY OF AUSTRALIA CIP DATA

Ellis, Ben, 1974–.
Falling petals.
rev. ed.
ISBN 9780868197845
I. Epidemics—Drama. I. Playbox Theatre (Melbourne, Vic.).
II. Title. (Series: Current theatre series).
A822.3

Typeset by Dean Nottle for Currency Press.
Cover design by Katy Wall for Currency Press.

Currency Press acknowledges the Traditional Owners of the Country on which we
live and work. We pay our respects to all Aboriginal and Torres Strait Islander
Elders, past and present.

Contents

Falling Ashes

John McCallum

This is a play from the front line of a new generation war. As a baby-boomer parent I'm not too happy with everything it has to say but it is extraordinarily powerful and its parable is alarmingly believable.

A generation that received a free liberal education decided to charge their children for training for jobs that kept disappearing. A generation brought up in a Keynesian world in which governments tried to regulate the conditions under which people could be exploited suddenly abandoned their children to wolves. A generation that celebrated the ideals of personal liberation, freedom and community created a world that they then allowed to be taken over by rapacious corporations. This is the world that Phil, Tania and Sally face so desperately in this play.

One of the hardest things for me is to watch Phil and Tania, the proto-fascist children who are the core of the play's story. These hard, cynical victims of the '90s have learned their lessons well: look out for yourself, jump through the hoops, crawl through sewers if necessary to do what you've been told you have to do in order to get what you've been told you ought to want. Everything they have been taught is bullshit—from the 'Mindpower' motivational programs to the new economics. They happily watch other children die, they torture their friend Sally when she gets sick, they have sex only because it helps them drill into their tightly-focussed minds a few of the rudimentary catchcries of the new orthodoxy that has ruined their community.

Ellis's other plays explore this bitter new generational crisis. In *Post Felicity* a baby-boomer couple are completely unable to acknowledge, let alone understand or care about, the disappearance of their daughter. Not even her death is enough to bring her to their lapsed attention. With the help of a mysterious employer they casually and brutally invent a new story for her and then dismiss her from their lives.

In *These People*, Ellis's response to the refugee scaremongering of the early 2000s, a traditional Australian family tries to deal with their fear of the aliens who are detained behind razor wire at the nearby detention centre. The Daughter of the family, writing an essay for school, captures the insanity of the world she is being raised in by creating a parable in which cute waddling penguins flee an eco-ravaged Antarctica and arrive on Australian shores seeking asylum. In a chilling moment one of the hungry penguins, played by the Daughter, is asked by a brutal detention centre guard to take off her penguin suit if she wants to eat. She does, and reveals underneath a woman in Islamic purdah, who has to keep undressing.

Ellis writes with a theatricality that is quite astonishing—a comic surrealism full of playful savagery and sudden shocks, all rooted in the real world that his characters and his audiences inhabit. It is, in Australian drama, a completely new way of writing about society and politics, based partly in powerful images: the penguins in *These People* and, in *Falling Petals*, the sakura tree under which the desperate and defiant children huddle. Each falling cherry-blossom represents another dead child. When the bodies are burned the falling blossoms are replaced by a rain of greasy ash that the surviving children cannot wipe off.

The strange disease that strikes Hollow, the ravaged country town from which Phil and Tania are so desperate to escape and to which Sally is condemned by her mother's poverty and intransigence, might be a metaphor for AIDS, or perhaps for the effects on ordinary people of economic rationalism, or perhaps for the New World Order. One of the smooth-talking evasive adults, Marg, calls it 'a truly postmodern disease'. The vital organs that it attacks survive individually but they suddenly stop co-operating with each other. The victims die from a failure, inside their own bodies, of community.

The plague ravages the town and the social fabric is torn and burnt. No-one understands what is going on. Families fail and parents and children stumble on blindly, calling on whatever friends they can find to give them support. The only close relationship is between Phil and Tania and the most savage moment in the play is when Phil abandons Tania to sexual slavery and crawls alone into the sewer that he believes will take him to the big city where he thinks he will be able do his exam and find his success.

The parents retreat happily to the safe country outside the fence that they have erected around the disaster area of the world that they have created for their children. The dying Sally, caught between two worlds, is left at the end, barely holding on but still fiercely defiant.

These three are part of the group in Hollow rejected, betrayed and destroyed at the very moment when the world should become theirs.

Falling Petals was first produced by Playbox Theatre at The C.U.B. Malthouse, Melbourne, on 2 July 2003 with the following cast:

TANIA	Caroline Craig
SALLY	Melia Naughton
PHIL	Paul Reichstein
MALE	James Wardlaw
FEMALE	Melita Jurisic

Director, Tom Healey
Designer, Anna Borghesi
Lighting Designer, Daniel Zika
Sound Design, David Franzke
Dramaturgical Consultant, Louise Gough

CHARACTERS

PHIL MOSS, 17

SALLY WOODS, 17

TANIA CARRIAGE, 17–18

A number of ADULT CHARACTERS (to be played by one male and one female actor.)

SETTING

The township of Hollow, population approximately 10,400 and rapidly declining. The present.

The action centres at a spot on the outskirts of this rural suburbia, part of a neglected (city-resident-owned) hobby farm, where a large tree, still alive and untouched by rising water tables or the persistent and almost permanent drought in the area, stands occasionally shedding petals. It is a cherry blossom tree, or 'sakura'. Most of the action takes place at this tree's trunk.

However, the action also spreads out around localities in the town, such as parts of the characters' homes, doctors' rooms and school offices, as indicated. This action takes place on the fringes of the sakura space, sometimes bleeding over it.

The 'sakura'—or the cherry blossom tree—in Japan is considered a very special tree, for it is the only tree there that blossoms in winter. In Hollow, an ongoing drought has confused it.

FIRST

At the sakura. Only part of a branch above is visible to the audience, plus part of the tree's trunk.

PHIL, TANIA *and* SALLY *are gathered there in school dress code—all shades of the one colour. The grass around them is brown-green-yellow.* PHIL *lies on the ground.* SALLY *is sitting up near him.* TANIA *is standing at the trunk, trying to shake the tree, but the trunk doesn't move.*

PHIL: Keep trying. It's ready to drop off, ready to cark it. Just like Vaughan. Bring him down and we'll have another funeral.

TANIA: A proper funeral.

> *She laughs and shakes the trunk.*

SALLY: Don't want another funeral today, thanks.

TANIA: What about tomorrow? We'll get us another day off.

PHIL: Here he comes. Woo-hoo!

> *A petal from above slowly floats down to the ground.*

TANIA: I did it!

PHIL: You didn't do anything. It was the forces of nature.

TANIA: We're all a part of nature and so anything we do is part of nature, so anything we do to nature is just nature taking its course.

PHIL: Please. You're letting Literature get too far into your head.

SALLY: [*to* PHIL] And you're letting Economics get way into yours.

PHIL: Economics gets me out of Hollow. Economics and Law, and in the long run, I might come back and buy a holiday house.

TANIA: In the long run, we are all dead.

PHIL: Keynes said that.

SALLY: Keynes is out of date.

PHIL: Mr Worboys likes him.

SALLY: Mr Worboys said that.

PHIL: Fucking alco.

TANIA: Do you reckon in the city they would let Mr Worboys teach?

PHIL: No way. [*He jumps up and scatters to the petal. He crosses himself like a priest.*] Dear Lord, please forgive the fallen for his sins—

SALLY: Phil, you're sick—

PHIL *picks up a handful of dirt-dust which he scatters upon the petal.*

PHIL: Ashes to ashes, dust to dust.

SALLY: Phil…

PHIL: See ya, Vaughan-y, baby!

SALLY: Stop it! We've had enough of that. Months of sickness.

PHIL: He was seven.

TANIA: That kid was sick before he was born.

PHIL: A real local.

SALLY: You're not even sorry for his mum? All the threats? People ringing up the house and being bastards over the phone?

PHIL: They're just the town of Hollow's Fuck Knuckles squad. Fuck Knuckles do Fuck Knuckly stuff.

SALLY: But to the mum of a sick kid? A dying kid?

TANIA: I heard he was a real shit, played it for sympathy.

PHIL: Dad taught him. Hated the kid. Trouble. [*Looking around*] Tania… I mean, [*crossing himself*] Vaughan's mother. Would you like to step up and say a few words about your son?

TANIA: [*wiping at her eyes*] Yes… yes, I will.

TANIA *laughs.*

SALLY: Oh, guys. Stop it.

TANIA: My boy… my boy… was a g-g-g-good boy! [*To* PHIL] Why did you take him away, God?

PHIL: [*still being the priest*] Hey, I only work for the guy.

TANIA: Oh, God! [*She gets down on her knees and beats the ground.*] Why did you take away my son? I w-w-w-w-waaaant him baaaaaack!

SALLY: It was nothing like that.

PHIL: It's close enough.

TANIA: [*still going*] Why me? Why will nobody give meeee a foot massssssage?

SALLY: She didn't say that.

PHIL: It's what she meant.

TANIA: [*wailing*] Foot massage! Foot massage!

PHIL *runs around and pulls* TANIA*'s leg.* TANIA *yelps and falls to the ground.* PHIL *pulls off her shoe.*

PHIL: Here's a foot massage.

He massages her foot.

2

TANIA: That tickles.

SALLY: How come I never get a foot massage, Phil?

Beat.

PHIL: Fuck, I hate this place. Can't wait to get out. Four more months.

SALLY: If you're unlucky.

TANIA: Did you see his practice exam marks, Sal?

SALLY: S'pose.

PHIL *starts tickling* TANIA*'s foot. She screams and scurries away.* PHIL *stands, crosses himself and stands over the petal.*

PHIL: Dearly aggrieved… Normally in times of distress I take off all of my clothes, grab a bottle of whisky, and dance around this chapel to 'Eagle Rock'. However, today there are people in attendance, and it's not even a Sunday. So, here's the next best thing. Blessed are the meek, for they shall inherit Vaughan's pitiful collection of CDs. Blessed are the poor in spirit, for the Central Hotel is just over the road. Let's bury this little shit and get tanked. Anyone into leather is especially welcome. Amen.

TANIA *is pissing herself laughing.* SALLY *just stares at the petal.*

SALLY: At the service I thought Vaughan was still breathing.

PHIL: You couldn't see the body. We were all put up the back.

SALLY: [*pointing to the petal*] Is he breathing?

TANIA: Yeah. Go up close to him and listen. Go on.

SALLY *stays still.*

SALLY: I'm not going near him.

TANIA: Hey, Sal, get a grip.

PHIL: Sally. That's not Vaughan's body. [*Beat.*] God, this place is small and nasty and fucked.

SALLY *moves again.*

TANIA: We're all in hick town.

SALLY: You're a hick, Tania.

TANIA: I'm moving out.

SALLY: With your practice exam marks, Tan?

TANIA: I wasn't motivated. I am now. You watch.

PHIL: I'm going to transcend this hickdom. Get into uni. Fuck off outta here.

SALLY: As if.

3

TANIA: That's right, Sally. No one leaves Hollow alive.

SALLY: Yeah, that's right, Phil. They end up dead.

The two girls converge slowly on PHIL.

PHIL: Hey, stop joking.

TANIA: No one leaves Hollow. The sickness gets you.

SALLY: And you never leave!

The two girls jump on PHIL *and wrestle him to the ground. He laughs, barely putting up a fight.*

[*Doing a Dracula*] I'm going to suck your blood!

TANIA: All of your organs will stop working and your brain will expand.

PHIL: Sounds like my study technique.

TANIA: And explode! Kaboom!

SALLY: It haemorrhaged.

PHIL: I'm going to transcend hickdom!

SALLY: Not if I can help it, mate.

TANIA runs and grabs the petal, while SALLY *holds a fairly comfortable* PHIL *down.*

TANIA: Here comes the sickness, Phil. Vaughan's special Hollow mystery illness!

She rushes at him with the petal, holding it in front of her. SALLY *sees the petal coming and jumps back in fright.*

SALLY: Don't fucking touch me with that. Fuck off.

TANIA: Okay. Hey, did you hear that three more kids might have that disease?

SALLY: Vaughan's disease?

PHIL: This has so freaked out Mum and Dad.

TANIA: [*laughing*] Yeah. Hasn't it?

SALLY: When?

TANIA: When I was round at Phil's place studying.

SALLY: When was that?

TANIA: Just some Economics stuff.

SALLY: Where was I?

PHIL: You don't want to go to uni, do you?

TANIA: Phil's mum and dad are like…

PHIL and TANIA put on falsely deep 'adult' voices.

PHIL: Terrible, terrible just watching a kid waste like that.

4

TANIA: The whole life a waste.

PHIL: Sometimes, you know, you see a kid dying, and you see them with a positive outlook, and you think, well, they had a nice life.

TANIA: But with this one, yes, it was all despair.

PHIL: Despair…

TANIA: The whole life, from start to finish, nothing enlightening about this death.

SALLY: Enlightening?

PHIL: I mean, you hope to find some hope in sick kids—

TANIA: But this kid knew—

PHIL: Stunted from the start—

SALLY: That's sick. The whole day's sick.

> PHIL *and* TANIA *drop the 'adult' bearings.*

TANIA: Hollow's sick. That's why it took the day off.

SALLY: Now three more kids have got it?

TANIA: Or something like it.

SALLY: Do you reckon it's contagious?

PHIL: It's just little kids; like mumps, isn't it?

TANIA: This place is a hole. Uni's going to be so cool.

SALLY: What's all this hating the place you come from all of a sudden?

PHIL: Look around you, Sally. We're nowhere.

SALLY: There's plenty to like. Plenty of space.

TANIA: Space, like outer space.

SALLY: Fresh air.

PHIL: [*sniffing*] Fresh is diesel and cow shit?

SALLY: You can't hate the place you come from. It's not natural.

PHIL: You know—tell any of the teachers that you want only the best results and only the best for yourself, and here—and only here— they knock you down. [*Impersonating a teacher*] Let's look over your tertiary choices… what's your name… Phil… and let's look— look, you've put Commerce-Law as your first choice. Why would you go and do a thing like that? Every three years, if we're lucky, we send a kid from this school to that course—and I really hope it's you—but pull your fucking head out of your arse—

TANIA: Are they allowed to say that?

PHIL: Look. I have to find kids jobs in supermarkets, service individual pathways, and if they want to do well in the supermarkets, then they ought to think about the local TAFE. What's your name again—

5

Phil—why haven't you put down a TAFE choice? You're cutting your own legs off. That won't help you walk down your pathway, cutting your own legs off.

TANIA: Did he really say all this?

PHIL: [*breaking out of it*] Yes— [*Back into it*] Now times have changed. If this was the sixties, maybe you might have been justified in making such a choice; I did. Look where it's got me. I'm a has-been. There's AIDS all over the place and I can't fuck as much anymore. So neither should you. I wish I was still a communist free-lover motherfucker, but you have responsibilities now. Take the supermarket job, Phil. Take it—

SALLY: He didn't say all of that.

PHIL: Maybe not all of it, no.

> *Beat.*

TANIA: Hollow is shit. Sandcastle is shit.

SALLY: Now, Sandcastle sucks. Hollow rocks.

> PHIL *laughs.*

TANIA: You've got to expand your horizons.

SALLY: Have you thought about how much it's all going to cost? Rent for one room is more than a four-bedroom up here!

TANIA: I've saved. I'll get a job.

PHIL: I'm happy. Mum took a package to leave teaching.

SALLY: Hollow has things that you can't get in the city. Hills. Fields. Clean air. Community and friendliness—most of us know what's going on for other people. Service clubs. We like that. We've got plenty of the kind of things that the city's got too. We've got a Maccas.

TANIA: You've got to be kidding.

SALLY: Don't you like Maccas?

PHIL: Jay-suss.

TANIA: Here, the definition of a new library book is one that's gone out of print in the last five years.

PHIL: We can't get the kind of school results we need unless we try twice as hard as the city kids.

SALLY: Well, if that's stopping you, maybe that's telling you something.

TANIA: Like what?

SALLY: You should stay here.

PHIL: Oh, crap. What it's telling us is this place is Nowhere Central. It's forgotten. It's not just forgotten, it's worth forgetting. It's failing. It's drought-ridden.

SALLY: We've always had droughts. Why should a smart kid from here run away to become a lawyer in the city? Or even become a lawyer to come back here to be one? How many lawyers do we need in Hollow?

TANIA: How many sheep get fucked?

SALLY: That was a one-off.

PHIL: Sal, why do you even bother to go to school at all when you don't want to go to uni?

SALLY: It's interesting.

PHIL: What?

SALLY: The subjects.

PHIL: What?

SALLY: The subjects are interesting.

PHIL: And?

SALLY: And what?

TANIA: Where will that get you?

SALLY: The subjects are interesting.

PHIL: So you've said, but what does that lead to?

SALLY: If they're interesting, they just are.

TANIA: For fuck's sake.

PHIL: Look. It's simple. How can you do good work, when you're not motivated? You won't get anywhere.

SALLY: Who said anything about getting anywhere?

PHIL: You just like being stupid.

SALLY: No, I don't.

PHIL: Aha! So you admit to being stupid!

SALLY *laughs.*

SALLY: I confess! You got me!

TANIA*'s mobile rings.*

TANIA: Ah fuck, what does Deano want? [*She answers it.*] Hello?

SALLY: [*to* PHIL] Phil, I think Economics is interesting.

PHIL: We need the marks to get to Melbourne, Sal. We have to get very intensive in our revision; spot-on definitions, clear graphs, succinct understandings. We can't just chase the 'interesting' bits and pieces around like butterflies.

7

SALLY: S'pose not.

PHIL: You don't want that kind of intensive revision. It would bore you. You don't need us.

SALLY: No.

PHIL: I'll miss you.

TANIA *finishes her call.*

TANIA: [*to* SALLY] Party.

SALLY: When?

TANIA: Saturday night. Deano's. We're invited.

PHIL: Really?

TANIA: Well. Sally and me.

SALLY: Deano wouldn't mind if you tagged along.

TANIA: He'll be surprised.

SALLY: You'll have to drink if you don't want to get bashed.

PHIL: Great. Never been bashed up before, but.

TANIA: So get drunk and sow some seeds instead, you big virgin.

TANIA *exits. Three more petals fall to the ground.*

SALLY: Three. Three more.

PHIL: Leave the little dead hicks alone.

◆ ◆ ◆ ◆ ◆

SECOND

At the sakura.

Two figures sit close together, either back-to-back or side-to-side, leaning against one another. It is night. Drought nights are clear nights, and it is a full moon. In the bluish dim light we see PHIL *and* TANIA. PHIL *switches on a dolphin torch. He shines it on the mound of petals.*

They are very drunk.

PHIL: Yep. Still there.

TANIA: You still spinning?

PHIL: Yep. Why did I come out tonight?

TANIA: It's a party.

PHIL: It's a crap party. It's a crap eighteenth.

8

TANIA: You could have at least put in for the present.

PHIL: Why should I? Deano won't be in Melbourne when I turn eighteen.

TANIA: S'pose not.

PHIL: And he listens to Troy Cassar-Daley. These are formative years. I'll have country music forever imprinted in my soul.

TANIA: Don't worry. In Psych, some say that your identity is infinitely flexible until you're around twenty. Identity links up with memory. So when you're no longer a 'country' boy, you won't remember the 'country' music.

PHIL: Thank Christ I've still got time.

TANIA: You fuckhead. What were you drinking?

PHIL: That spumante shit.

TANIA: Should have done the shots of vodka.

PHIL: But that doesn't taste of anything. Does it?

TANIA: Dunno. Had it with cordial.

PHIL: Yuck. I don't want to lose brain cells.

TANIA: You've got plenty left over.

PHIL: But have I? Troy Cassar-Daley, for crying out loud.

TANIA: Some country music is all right.

PHIL: No. Nothing good can come of it. They don't have it in Melbourne.

TANIA: They have shops full of country music in Melbourne.

PHIL: And other stuff. That's the point. There's other stuff. There's choice.

TANIA: I like Troy Cassar-Daley.

PHIL: Then why did you leave the party?

TANIA: There are other things I like.

PHIL: Like what?

TANIA: I like the idea of you being on your own out here.

PHIL: Leave me alone, then. Let me study the effects of flashlight on flora. What's happened to Sally?

Silence.

Tania.

TANIA: What?

PHIL: Have… have you completed your tertiary choices form?

TANIA: What do you reckon?

PHIL: Did you get it past Mr Syme?

TANIA: *Mais oui.*

PHIL: Did he give you shit?

TANIA: Of course he did. 'You might like eating pie-in-the-sky, but down here on Earth you have to earn a living. Look, it's great to have dreams, I dream of Jeannie, but in reality I have to make sure that your needs are met.'

PHIL: Really?

TANIA: Yep.

PHIL: Imagine if he told that to a kid at Melbourne Grammar. Needs.

TANIA: Wouldn't get away with it.

PHIL: And?

TANIA: And what?

PHIL: Did you get it past him?

TANIA: It's my choices.

PHIL: Choices. Yes. Good. [*Beat.*] You put Melbourne at the top.

TANIA: Yes.

PHIL: You didn't put any TAFE in it.

TANIA: No.

PHIL: Just wanted to make sure.

TANIA: It's going to happen, Phil.

PHIL: Yeah.

TANIA: You, me, Melbourne, a flat.

PHIL: Eventually I want something by myself.

TANIA: Really?

PHIL: I like the idea of a studio apartment. Have you been reading the classifieds?

TANIA: Not really.

PHIL: You have to, Tan. There are classifieds, and there are houses and flats for rent. At first, maybe I'll share with other people, maybe including you. But when I get established I can get a studio apartment. Everything in the one place.

TANIA: That's all you'd come home to.

PHIL: There'd be work, too. There's places open after six in Melbourne. Places that are open all night. Home would be just a place to sleep.

TANIA: You can have fun at home.

PHIL: But there's a choice.

Beat.

TANIA: It's going to happen, Phil.

PHIL: Really? You'll do well.

TANIA: Everybody is capable of anything. With positive thinking especially. Only three per cent of people write down their goals; but of those who do, they achieve eighty per cent of them.

PHIL: Is that true?

TANIA: Listen to the MindPower CDs, read the booklet. It's all in there. It's changed my life.

Footsteps.

Shh.

PHIL: Who's there.

SALLY: [*from offstage*] Me.

SALLY *enters and steps into the mound of petals which* PHIL*'s torch continues to illuminate.*

Shit.

PHIL *slowly trails the torchlight up from her feet to her face. She is looking down at the ground. She is very drunk.*

TANIA: You stepped on your petals, Sal.

SALLY: It's terrible. How could I do such a thing? They're just children. I'm just pissed. It's not my fault. They were there. And now I've stepped on them. Crunch, splosh, crunch crunch the kiddies—

TANIA: It's all right, Sal—

SALLY: No, it's not—

TANIA: Come here and sober up—

SALLY: I'm ruining them forever—

She starts to cry.

TANIA: Phil, take that torch off her face.

PHIL: No. She's entertaining me.

SALLY: [*crying*] I stepped on them.

PHIL: She is so pissed.

TANIA: So are you.

PHIL: You're pissed, aren't you, Sally?

SALLY: Yes, I'm pissed.

TANIA: It's okay, Sal. It's only blossom.

SALLY: But I stepped on them.

TANIA *gets up, goes to her, hugs her and tries to shush her.*

I drank too much at the start. I just spent the last thirty minutes wandering out of town to get here. Before that I didn't know where

11

you'd gone. I didn't know. And I spent half an hour with my eyes shut pashing the wrong bloke. I turned to get my drink and felt his hand on my face and I thought it was him…

PHIL: Thought it was something like that.

SALLY: I stepped *in* them.

TANIA: It's okay, Sal.

SALLY: My feet stink.

PHIL: Of what—pot pourri?

SALLY *bursts into tears.*

TANIA: Stop being mean to her.

PHIL: Well, she's the one upset about it.

TANIA: She's drunk and in heels. She's got a right.

SALLY *still cries.*

SALLY: I was alone.

PHIL *switches off the torch.*

PHIL: It's all right. When we're in Melbourne, it'll be just like this. Get used to it. You'll be alone / all the time.

TANIA: [*overlapping*] Phil—what's that? / Can you hear that?

TANIA *grabs the torch off him and turns it on the tree.*

PHIL: [*overlapping*] But you'll be able to get pissed, pash plenty of wrong blokes and then stumble like a slut up the highway, it's only a four-and-a-half-day walk to Melbourne. If you fuck some speeding trucker you might get there in five or six hours, if he's going the same way. But we'll be there, Sal. Don't forget that we'll be there at the end. Just like tonight.

TANIA *points the torch at the branches above. A petal falls down. She follows the trajectory.*

TANIA: See, Sal. There's always more.

SALLY: Who is it now?

PHIL: What?

SALLY: Which one of the little bastards died now?

TANIA: Come on. There's only been three deaths. It's just coincidence. That's what the paper said.

SALLY: It's another one. Another one's dead. Hey, Phil. You should have stayed at the party.

PHIL: With those losers?

SALLY: There were some pretty Year Elevens. Talking about which, one of them was going to fuck you.

TANIA: [*laughing*] Really?

SALLY: They wanted to hold a virgin raffle.

> TANIA *cackles.*

You should have stayed. Could have got your rocks off. Learnt what it's really all about. Another one's dead. Which one of the little fucking kiddies is gone now?

◆ ◆ ◆ ◆ ◆

THIRD

In this section, the action breaks out all over town, and incorporates the two other actors as various 'adult' personages. As indicated.

◆ ◆ ◆ ◆ ◆

In the general practice of DR GEORGE FRANZ. *There is a local journo with him,* SARAH GODDEN.

GODDEN: So three more kids have died—

FRANZ: Yes—

GODDEN: And it's from the same thing, but—

FRANZ: It appears—

GODDEN: But you're not ready to call it a disease.

FRANZ: We don't know what it is, that's what I'm telling you.

GODDEN: But it's the same thing.

FRANZ: All the patients died displaying similar symptoms.

GODDEN: But?

FRANZ: From differing complications.

GODDEN: So they died of the same thing or not? What do I put in the paper?

FRANZ: Okay. Once more. They all displayed similar, almost exact symptoms, but the exact causes of death were different in each case. What happened before each death was this. First, a rash appears.

13

GODDEN: So parents should report any rashes to you?

FRANZ: I don't want to cause any unnecessary hysteria. But it would be a good idea, if it is accompanied by flu-like aches and pains.

GODDEN: And anything else?

FRANZ: You'd think there was some simple virus—don't quote me that it might be a virus. Don't even quote me as saying it might be blood-borne.

GODDEN: It's neither?

FRANZ: Of course it could be either. That's how little we know of the causes. What I do know and have observed is the following—now you can quote me.

GODDEN: Gee, thanks.

FRANZ: The organs of the body stop working for the body.

GODDEN: Wouldn't that mean an instant death?

FRANZ: Normally. But it's about two weeks to four months. So far. In that period, these organs appear to work—if you examine each in isolation. That's what had me stumped with the first one. You get the test results back for individual organs and you'd think, well, it's a little bit down, but that wouldn't cause *this*. But what seems to happen is that the organs do enough to make themselves function.

GODDEN: What's the problem then?

FRANZ: Well, they're a part of a system. You can't have kidneys just purifying blood for the kidneys. They have to do it for the body. And in this, this…

GODDEN: Child-ridding disease…

FRANZ: For God's sake, don't call it that.

GODDEN: Only the kids are getting it.

FRANZ: That sounds awful.

GODDEN: That's the headline. So—

FRANZ: It could be a bacteria, disease, infection—I don't know yet.

GODDEN: Tell me when you find out and I'll change the headline.

FRANZ: Gee.

GODDEN: So—after that?

FRANZ: After what?

GODDEN: The kidneys. Blood. Purifying. What goes wrong?

FRANZ: A body can't sustain itself if the organs are working selectively. And they seem to get more and more selective. Depending on which part of the body you take the blood from, there are different counts of white cells. You don't normally get that. And in a cancer or an immunosuppressant virus you often get the majority of white cells turning bad, whereas in these cases it sort of… spreads.

GODDEN: I can't seem to make a good quote out of that.

FRANZ: Don't call it a child-ridding disease.

GODDEN: Why not?

FRANZ: I've heard around the village that you want to get back into Melbourne. This is not a story to try and make your name with.

GODDEN: Haven't made up my mind. 'Townspeople standing up in times of tragedy.' Or 'town in fear of mystery illness'.

FRANZ: Child-ridding… it's just… You don't have to write this. The town doesn't need it. You lot don't report the local crime. You don't have to report the local illness.

GODDEN: Here's my card. When the story breaks, the sharks who'll descend from Melbourne and Sydney to pounce on my turf will be ringing you when you're trying to sleep. You'll need someone like me to refer them to. Help you deal with all the attention.

FRANZ: I'll try to get you more information if you hold off for a few weeks.

GODDEN *considers it.*

GODDEN: All right. For a while. But it had better not break anywhere else. Or you'll really owe me. [*Pause.*] Have any more children come down with the child-ridding disease?

FRANZ: I told you. I don't even know if it is a disease.

GODDEN *exits.*

◆ ◆ ◆ ◆ ◆

SALLY *enters the consulting room.*

SALLY: Reception said I could see you now.

FRANZ: Hello, Sally. What's your poison?

SALLY: Just a prescription for the pill.

FRANZ: I'll need to take your blood pressure then.

SALLY: You did that last time. Last time you said only every six months. All I need is a prescription.

FRANZ: Why don't you lie down?

SALLY: I'd rather just get the prescription and go.

15

FRANZ: So you've got good use out of the first? You should think about having a pap smear soon. [*He writes out a script, tears it off, but holds onto it.*] By the way. You might want to watch out for some symptoms that are going around town. Any speckled rash on the upper arms. Listlessness. Uncontrollable urge to suck in lots of air. You come see me straight away.

SALLY: Why do you think I should watch out for those symptoms?

FRANZ: I'll take your blood pressure.

SALLY: Do you think I have their sickness?

FRANZ: It's actually a syndrome, because it's a collection of symptoms, with no as yet identified cause. I'm going to give it a name.

SALLY: You don't think I have it, do you?

FRANZ: The Hollow Syndrome? No, no, but blood pressure and a pap smear might help warn us.

SALLY: No pap smear.

FRANZ: Your pressure's up a little.

SALLY: What?

FRANZ: I'll take it again. Relax and think of it as another exam to pass. Relax. Good. Where are you planning to study next year?

SALLY: Nowhere. In the shop.

FRANZ: Smart girl like you? Not going to university?

SALLY: Can't afford it.

FRANZ: There's, what, youth allowance.

SALLY: Get that if I stay here and I don't have to pay rent. Besides, there's HECS.

FRANZ: That's for later.

SALLY: No. It's not. It's for now, and it costs more if you can't afford it.

FRANZ: Hmm. Not how I understood it.

SALLY: What was the second reading?

FRANZ: It's fine. Here's your script. I'll bulk bill you for this one. No need for your mother to ask questions about her account with us. She doesn't need to know.

SALLY: She knows.

FRANZ: That's enlightened for this place. I'll fix up the bulk billing with reception. In your own time.

    FRANZ *leaves.*

◆ ◆ ◆ ◆ ◆

The space becomes Sally's room. She holds the script, looking at it. She looks at her upper arms in turn. She peers at every freckle as a potential abnormality.

SALLY*'s mother,* MRS WOODS, *enters. She is holding a pair of pants, which are inside-out, and is threading them.*

WOODS: Sal, do you want to help me with any of this? Or do you just want to sit on your arse all night? Did you eat?

SALLY: No, Mum.

WOODS: Sal, do you want to help me fix up any of the trousers? There's plenty of trouser work this week.

SALLY: I'm studying, Mum.

WOODS: Funny way to study, staring at a piece of paper. It's only taking-up. Come on.

Silence.

What's got into you?

SALLY *slowly ambles past her mother, out of the room.*

Suits me. Go and study then. I'll keep the roof over your head. I'll do the taking-up. I'll keep the business running. Don't mind me.

◆ ◆ ◆ ◆ ◆

MRS WOODS *finishes mending the trousers. Around her, the setting becomes the school library, for Hollow Secondary's parent-teacher night. It is large enough to hold a parent-teacher night because there are so few books in the building.*

MR SYME *sets up.*

SYME: Is it our appointment now, Mrs Woods?

WOODS: I brought your trousers in, Gordon.

SYME: Right.

WOODS: Don't pay me here. I'll put you on account at the shop.

SYME: How is that little arcade?

WOODS: Little. Take the trousers then.

SYME: Right. Sally's doing well.

WOODS: Good to hear. What's she doing wrong?

SYME: Not much. She's a very bright student, Mrs Woods. In my Human Development class, well, she is close to excelling.

WOODS: You're talking about Sally?

SYME: Yes. But there's only one small problem.

WOODS: Oh.

SYME: As careers guidance supervisor, I have to check all the tertiary admissions forms—

WOODS: Tertiary?

SYME: TAFE and university.

WOODS: University?

SYME: Sally hasn't handed one in yet.

WOODS: Good girl.

SYME: Pardon?

WOODS: Won't be necessary, Mr Syme.

SYME: I think it would be a good idea for Sally to pursue some kind of further study. Suited to her needs. Now, the local TAFE offers an excellent—

WOODS: And how much does that cost?

SYME: There are reasonable—

WOODS: Look, Mr Syme, me and Sally, I sat her down two years ago when she talked about uni and I showed her the maths, and she and I came to a decision—it costs too much. She agrees with me.

SYME: I'm only suggesting that she keep her options open.

WOODS: We've talked about them and there are none. She just needs her Matric.

SYME: In your day, maybe, Mrs Woods, it was called Matric and that was a big qualification.

WOODS: In my day? In my day?

SYME: In our day.

WOODS: Next time you come to the shop, you'd better pay for those pants. [*Preparing to leave*] I don't run a credit company. Just a very small business.

She gets out of there.

◆ ◆ ◆ ◆ ◆

Still the parent-teacher night. MR SYME *is slightly baffled.* PHIL *enters, carrying some essays. He goes straight up to* MR SYME.

SYME: Hello… is your mum in next… what's your…?

PHIL: It's Phil.

SYME: Yes.

PHIL: You don't teach me.

SYME: Right.

PHIL: See this?

SYME: A practice exam paper.

PHIL: 'A'.

SYME: Where's your father, then?

PHIL: Doing a lesson plan for tomorrow. Grief Counselling for Grade Two.

SYME: You're the Moss boy.

PHIL: It's Phil. Look at this one. What mark does it have?

SYME: 'A' plus.

PHIL: Pretty good, eh? And this one.

SYME: 'A'.

PHIL: And this?

SYME: 'A' minus.

PHIL: And here?

SYME: Eighty-nine per cent.

PHIL: Now—you tell me to take my fucking head out of my arse.

SYME: What?

PHIL: Look at my results.

SYME: Right. Excellent.

PHIL: You pull your own head out of your fucking arse and tell me again that I can't make Commerce or Commerce-Law at Melbourne.

SYME: They are good practice exam results. And practice exams can be different from the final marked ones. You need to remember, should you not achieve those results—

PHIL: They are the beginning, you cunt. You call yourself career guidance. You ought to be sacked. I am not some fucking hick with a pointless life full of pointless TAFE to look forward to. Look at the results and tell me again what sort of student I am.

Silence.

You're a cunt.

SYME *leaves.*

◆ ◆ ◆ ◆ ◆

PHIL *stays. And it's now the home of the Mosses.* GAYLE MOSS *is coming home late from working.*

GAYLE: How did the chat with all the teachers go?

PHIL: Really well. They were a bit put out that you and Dad didn't go.

GAYLE: I did tell them. You're a mature adult.

PHIL: Yes. I got the practice exams I wrote back.

GAYLE: Good. What were the comments?

PHIL: I didn't read the comments.

GAYLE: Phil—you ought to read the comments.

PHIL: The marks are the comments, Mum. I know what I'm doing here.

GAYLE: Really.

PHIL: I'll read you one of my essays.

GAYLE: Not now, Phil. I've just come home.

PHIL: No. Let me. You'll like it.

GAYLE: Maybe later.

PHIL: It's not exactly a bedtime story, Mum.

GAYLE: Look—Vaughan's mother came into the store today, and it just reminded me what happens with this sickness that's getting some of the little ones.

PHIL: What, the parents grieve?

GAYLE: Phil! Don't let your father hear you talk like that. He's losing sleep over this.

PHIL: And little students.

GAYLE: Phil, don't be like that. It's a tragedy.

PHIL: 'Small children come down with a sickness in order to skip father's boring primary school class, and die accidentally. Is this a tragedy?' Discuss.

GAYLE: Phil! That's rude and unattractive.

PHIL: I'm better looking than a corpse. Oh—I forgot. This town just loves a little corpse—so sweet, so gentle, so at peace. Pop on a floral arrangement and Bob's your uncle. Such bullshit.

GAYLE: Please.

PHIL: Where's your sense of humour?

GAYLE: I saw Vaughan's mother, for crying out loud, Phil. How do you think she feels at the moment? Try to see it from her point of view.

PHIL: [*squinting*] Nup. Not much.

GAYLE: Phil!

PHIL: But I can hear an echo when she's thinking. Not much up top in Hollow skulls.

GAYLE: You're not a parent. You can't understand what it's like.

PHIL: Parent?! These parents, these stupid National Party- and One Nation-Liberal-voting cocksuckers complain about money so much that you'd think they'd be happy not to have kids anymore.

GAYLE: These parents are in agony, Phil.

PHIL: And the little shits are in more.

GAYLE: Huh!

PHIL: Let me read you my essay. It's about microeconomic reform.

GAYLE: No.

PHIL: Oh, come on. You'll enjoy it. You can give me comments.

GAYLE: Phil. I have just come home from work. I have to go to the toilet.

PHIL: That's all right. I'll read it to you through the door. It's a pisser.

GAYLE: No, Phil. No.

PHIL: Big voice, Mum. That's what you always say. Big voice.

GAYLE: Let me go to the toilet, Phil.

PHIL: It's the economics part of it, isn't it?

GAYLE: Phil!

PHIL: What about my fabulous English argumentative essay? About accepting change.

GAYLE: No.

> GAYLE *exits.*

PHIL: [*shouting after her*] What's the matter? Failed hippy parent stuck in the country with a son who can see reality for what it is? Come on! I'm your son. You must have had something to do with it. I'll shout you the economics essay.

◆ ◆ ◆ ◆ ◆

TANIA *is at the tree.* PHIL *walks to her as she speaks. She is laughing.*

TANIA: Did she say anything after that?

PHIL: No. But at first I heard her piddling, then I heard her crying. Stupid cow.

TANIA: Mad cow.

PHIL: Worse.

TANIA: Your mum's all right, though. For an ex-hippy.

PHIL: Fucking hippies. Fucking Kombi van. You'd think they could get rid of that shit heap at least. Buy something new.

TANIA: Mmm. I love the smell of new cars.

PHIL: You can get that smell in a can, apparently.

TANIA: Really?

PHIL: Yeah.

TANIA: And you can spray it on the hippies that pass you in the street?

PHIL: Yeah!

TANIA: Fucking hippies. They are so out of touch. When my grandfather came back from Vietnam, he—

PHIL: Your grandad fought in Vietnam?

TANIA: Yeah—lost an arm.

PHIL: Shit.

TANIA: But when he got back, there was no parade, and just fucking hippies spitting on him in the street.

PHIL: Wow.

TANIA: No wonder he got onto the smack. The hippies got him on the hammer.

PHIL: Hang on. Didn't he lose an arm?

TANIA: Yes.

PHIL: So, if he was on the gear, how did he shoot up?

TANIA: I don't know. He taught me how to clean a gun. Could do that with one arm.

PHIL: Sounds kind of cool.

TANIA: Scary, more like.

PHIL: I wonder if the guy who bought this place off us will ever come and clean it up.

TANIA: He's from the city, isn't he?

PHIL: Yeah. Wanted it for a hobby farm. And weekends.

TANIA: What a dickhead.

PHIL: Took three minutes to kill all the sheep. Doesn't seem like he came back since.

TANIA: City people think it's all easy out here.

PHIL: This guy did, I suppose. I don't know. Mum and Dad still lost money out of the sale. Hippies in Capitalism.

TANIA: Hey, mannnn. Like, let's go to the country and be, like, alternative, man.

PHIL: Is that the best you can do?

TANIA: And we'll, like, wear bells on our toes and plant dope and invite all the dolphins to the river, and we'll have a, like, dolphin orgeeee. Should shoot the lot of them.

PHIL: Weak bastards'll just all die out eventually. Like those stupid little bastard kids.

TANIA: Sucked up too much dirt and got some Abo curse, I reckon.

PHIL: Nothing to do with that. They've just got no ambition to live. That's all. How many?

TANIA: Twenty.

A petal falls.

PHIL: No. Twenty-one.

The lights go out on the two little proto-fascists.

◆ ◆ ◆ ◆ ◆

MALCOLM MULVANEY appears. He is the Hollow Chamber of Commerce President. He motions to calm down a meeting.

MULVANEY: Order, order. I hereby open this extraordinary general meeting of the Hollow and Districts Chamber of Commerce. It is obvious that we have a small health problem in this area concerning some of the young ones, and that some of us have concerns that this may impact on bookings for the upcoming tourist season. There may be questions from the media. So what I have developed here is a media statement to refer you to. The Chamber exec has developed it, and I think you will agree it is a very fine piece of work. But before you read, I'll give you the gist. Now, just imagine, if the worst comes to the worst and I have to front some tiny media pack, we arrange this…

Up comes Malcolm Mulvaney, President, and I say, of course we are worried as locals by the naming of this unspeakable child-ridding disease as the Hollow Syndrome, and that a drop in bookings may result. But holiday makers should realise that so far no cause has been determined and it is only Hollow children who are affected.

The point I want to get across to people is that Hollow is still a bloody good place! There is no reason to associate us with this problem. And we're working on it. Hollow is your average, fine, typical, relaxing, beautiful countryside town that you can still take the family to. [*Sweeping an arm out*] See? Even with the drought, it still possesses a stirring and striking Australian landscape. Think, people, of Hollow as being like something out of *Seachange*, but cheaper, huge industrial potential, and with a picturesque river instead.

An interruption.

What?

He pauses for a question.

Has there been any metropolitan interest following the report, was the question.

No. No bites yet. It seems to be going mostly unreported to my knowledge. Which is a fantastic result.

◆ ◆ ◆ ◆ ◆

FOURTH

At the tree area.

PHIL *and* TANIA *are lying back, looking up at the tree branches.* SALLY *is a little bit away from them, holding two twigs, attempting to push one into the ground to make a cross.* SALLY *is doing this at the mound of petals she stepped on earlier.*

PHIL: [*not looking at her*] Give it up, Sally.

SALLY *keeps on trying.*

TANIA: Here comes another one!

PHIL: Who, who is it this time?

TANIA: Little Simon!

PHIL: A-ha! Come on, Simon. Down you drop.

TANIA: Ring-a-rosey!

A petal falls. PHIL *and* TANIA *jump up and point at it, following its trajectory.*

PHIL: No more school for you, Simon!

SALLY: You guys are sick.

TANIA: No, Simon is!

PHIL: Was!

> *The petal is still falling.* PHIL *and* TANIA *hold their breaths. The petal lands.* PHIL *and* TANIA *burst out laughing.*

Another one bites the dust.

TANIA: [*picking the petal up*] Do you want another one for your collection, Sal?

SALLY: Fuck off.

PHIL: We gotta relax somehow. Swot-vac soon.

TANIA: It's so unfair—

SALLY: I thought you wanted the exams to come.

TANIA: Unfair of the kids to die. It's like they want us to fail.

> SALLY *breaks the twig she is trying to push in.*

SALLY: Damn!

> TANIA *giggles at her.*

PHIL: 'S all right, Sal.

SALLY: Gawd, I'm even too stupid to make a marker.

PHIL: Why worry 'bout yourself so much, Sal?

TANIA: You're not stupid.

PHIL: No… it's the stupid children you should be concerned with.

TANIA: The children, the children.

SALLY: How would you like it if it was you?

PHIL: It's not going to be.

TANIA: Oh, the children, the children. Sing along, everybody.

PHIL: Oh, the children, the children. We mourn for the children.

SALLY: Don't be so mean.

PHIL: I'm hungry.

> *He grabs an apple out of his school bag. He bites into it. He notices that the apple is rotten and spits out his mouthful.*

Oh, that's disgusting.

> TANIA *laughs at him.*

TANIA: And there's a worm in it.

PHIL: Oh, Jesus.

> *He tosses it at the tree trunk.*

TANIA: This place is so sick it can't even grow good apples!

SALLY: An apple a day keeps the doctor away, because the worms will eat you instead?

PHIL: Fuck off. Sally Hick. Hick Girl.

SALLY: Just because I'm not like you.

PHIL: Just because you're a fucking Bush Pig. Oink-oink.

SALLY: Bush Pigs live out of town. I live east of the shops! I'm not a Bush Pig like those girls at school from Barker. I'm from town.

PHIL: Hollow's a town, a country town, all country is Bush Pig Country!

SALLY: Hollow's a decent-sized, normal rural centre.

TANIA: Oh, yeah? How many kids cark it in other regions?

PHIL: Bring on the statistics. Bring 'em on.

SALLY: That's just an abnormality.

PHIL: Abnormal is as abnormal does.

TANIA: And what about that dickbrain going on about the effects of tourism and never saying what's really going on?

SALLY: They're worried for the businesses. It's natural.

TANIA: Bit of truth wouldn't go astray.

SALLY: You can't take the views of a few Hollow people and say that the whole place is shit.

PHIL: It's Hollow's fault. Something about the place.

TANIA: Yeah. All those burning mattresses on the nature strips. It's getting out of hand.

SALLY: That's just a couple of hooligans.

TANIA: Cops aren't doing anything about it. Seen them watching on, clapping.

PHIL: And the rocks they piff at the sick kids' roofs? What about them?

SALLY: It's hard not to get caught up in all of it.

TANIA: Couldn't get out on the street today. Was so packed.

SALLY: You've got a sickie near you?

TANIA: Four doors down.

PHIL: Same. Three doors.

SALLY: Well, I'm lucky, but there is one around the corner.

PHIL: It's the way the crowds mass and salivate. You wouldn't get salivation in Melbourne. The cops'd do something because of the media.

Beat.

SALLY: How many rocks have you piffed?

Beat.

TANIA: A few.
SALLY: Same.
PHIL: Same.
SALLY: It's easy to get carried away.

◆ ◆ ◆ ◆ ◆

FIFTH

Two scenes run concurrently in this section.

Right, is Phil's home; left, is Sally's home.

JOHN MOSS *and* MRS WOODS *await their children in their respective spaces.*
MRS WOODS *holds a blanket.* MR MOSS *wears a pained expression.*

Both PHIL *and* SALLY *are getting up for breakfast.*

◆ ◆ ◆ ◆ ◆

PHIL'S STORY...

PHIL *enters.*

JOHN: You might want to go back to bed, son.
PHIL: Hmmn?
JOHN: Why don't you take it easy today? Get some rest?
PHIL: I've got school. So have you.
JOHN: Have a few days off on me.
PHIL: Dad, I've got Accounting today. I want to make up the numbers.
JOHN: You won't be able to.
PHIL: Why didn't you laugh?
JOHN: After breakfast, just have a lie in. A sleep in. A lie down.
PHIL: Are you okay?
JOHN: It's important.
PHIL: Have you finally gone insane, Dad?
JOHN: Schools are closed. A whole bunch of high school kids came down
    with the Syndrome. Couple of them went.
PHIL: A whole bunch?
JOHN: A quarter of the high school have got it.
PHIL: That'll be the stupid kids then, won't it?

27

JOHN: Phil.

PHIL: The dumb kids. That's good. Any final year kids? Dumb kids bring down the mean. Dumb kids bring down the marks. I hope there were final year kids.

JOHN: It's hard for you Phil, I know. Be strong.

PHIL: I am. I'm going to get out of here. Quick. Ring up the Principal in Sandcastle—I'll finish the year out there.

JOHN: Can't do that.

PHIL: What? You mean you don't want to do it.

JOHN: You can't go to Sandcastle.

PHIL: You're an arsehole, Dad.

JOHN: The area's been quarantined.

PHIL: What?!

JOHN: Until the Syndrome... blows over... or they understand what causes or transmits it.

PHIL: And the school's closed until then.

JOHN: Phil. Won't you have friends who...?

PHIL: Don't lay the guilt trip on me, Dad. I've got enough to worry about. What's going to happen to our exams?

JOHN: You should be thinking about the value of human life at a time like this. What you would like to do—?

PHIL: And my life? Some dumb, unambitious tools get terminal—and my life is being destroyed? Value of human life? These are Hollow hicks keeling over, Dad, making my school close down! It's probably some in-bred thing going back generations.

JOHN: Phil?

PHIL: No ambition, no future, no bigger picture, that's why they're dying. Worthless deaths—that's not a tragedy! You talk all you like about the value of their lives and forget about me, then. I've got to get my ticket: it's called university entrance.

JOHN: You're stressed. You don't mean that.

PHIL: Fuck yeah, I'm stressed. This had better not be a joke, Dad.

JOHN: It's not a joke.

PHIL: So they know nothing about this Syndrome and they just decide to lock us away here, miles from anywhere.

JOHN: We're not miles from anywhere; we're here.

PHIL: You're the bloody primary teacher. It started with primary school kids. Maybe you're the carrier. Maybe they ought to lock you up.

JOHN: Don't talk like that.

PHIL: Are they still paying your wages?

JOHN: Don't talk like this. Phil. What have I brought you up to believe in?

PHIL: Get fucked.

JOHN *leaves.*

Every problem is not a problem. It's a challenge. This is a challenge. A challenge that shall make the end result all the sweeter. A challenge is an opportunity. Lie of Success.

He goes to a stereo and turns on a tape.

TAPE: [*voice-over*] Lie of Success. Number Two. Everything happens for a reason. There is no good or bad, only results. If there is any Lie of Success you need to believe more than any other in my MindPower series, it is this one.

PHIL: Everything happens for a reason.

TAPE: [*voice-over*] It is amazing, I have found in my life, what happens when you apply this belief to any situation that you previously may have found dispiriting. It's the belief that I credit with my global success today.

PHIL: Global— [*He switches the tape off.*] Time to study.

◆ ◆ ◆ ◆ ◆

SALLY'S STORY

SALLY *enters.*

WOODS: Morning.

SALLY: Hey, Mum.

WOODS: Time to talk.

SALLY: I'm running late.

WOODS: You're not running anywhere today.

SALLY: It's not Saturday, yet. I've got school.

WOODS: School's closed.

SALLY: No.

WOODS: Was on the radio.

SALLY: Wasn't on Triple J.

WOODS: Was on the local.

SALLY: Why?

WOODS: Sounds like about twenty high school kids died last night.

SALLY: Oh.

WOODS: It's not good, Sal.

SALLY: No. No.

WOODS: So they've closed the school and quarantined the town.

SALLY: What. What are they doing?

WOODS: They want to work out what's causing it.

SALLY: I thought only little kids could get it. Was there… anyone I know?

WOODS: Presume the parents would have rung you up. [*Beat.*] It's time, Sally.

SALLY: Time for what?

WOODS: Time you moved on.

SALLY: And worked in the shop. Okay.

WOODS: No. It's time you moved on.

SALLY: What?

WOODS: You were always going to be kicked out by the end of the year. Let you become an adult by going out on your own. But now business demands that you go.

SALLY: Mum, are you all right?

WOODS: Here's a blanket.

SALLY: Where am I going to sleep?

WOODS: I'm giving you a blanket. The business can't afford more. My customers know that I have a child at the high school. Now nobody is saying how this Syndrome gets passed around, but I'm not taking any chances. I don't want people attacking my shop.

SALLY: No one's attacked your shop, Mum. I'm not sick.

WOODS: Can't take the chance. Have to stop it before it starts. I'll be assuring my customers that you haven't touched any of their clothes before taking this step.

SALLY: Mum.

WOODS: Look, it's not what I would want to do, but I don't know much about anything, and anything might be causing this disease. Better to be safe.

SALLY: Mum.

WOODS: Come on. Get out. Out you go.

SALLY: Mum?

WOODS: There's a drought on. It'll still be warm at night.

SALLY: You want this.

WOODS: There's no alternative. I'm not making the choices. Don't make this any harder.

> SALLY *stares at her mother for a beat, and then takes the blanket from her. She leaves.*

◆ ◆ ◆ ◆ ◆

SIXTH

At the tree.

SALLY *is sitting at the tree trunk, blanket under her arm.*

PHIL *enters, carrying a plastic bag. He drops it at his own feet.*

PHIL: Brought you some stuff.

SALLY: Gee, thanks.

PHIL: You're not authorised.

SALLY: What's unauthorised about me?

PHIL: The sign says authorised entry only. I'm taking a risk for you.

> TANIA *enters, also carrying a plastic bag.*

Be thankful we managed to make it through.

TANIA: Stole this from Dad's truck. Phil.

PHIL: What?

TANIA: You've got dirty, black dandruff.

PHIL: Fuck off. Hey, Sal, have you heard?

SALLY: What?

PHIL: This is great.

TANIA: What is it?

PHIL: They're burning the bodies. All the dead bastards are getting chucked on pyres.

> *He is laughing. Black ashes begin to fall from the sky.*

TANIA: [*laughing*] They should just leave nature to it to sort it all out.

SALLY: Sure.

TANIA: It's going to blow over, Sal, you frigging hobo. Cheer up.

PHIL: [*laughing*] Have a sense of humour. It's pretty funny. You getting kicked out by your mum.

31

TANIA: Come on. You gotta laugh.

PHIL: [*scratching his head*] They don't guard this perimeter very well. City Boy must be getting paid a fortune for letting the Authorities use this place.

TANIA: They're using this place?

PHIL: They're burning the bodies just over there.

TANIA: [*laughing*] Shit! No kidding!

SALLY: My blanket's getting dirtier.

TANIA: Phil. All your dandruff. You should shower.

PHIL: Fuck off.

TANIA: [*looking up*] Oh, hang on.

> *She starts laughing hysterically.*

PHIL: What is it?

TANIA: [*barely controlled*] It's the ashes! It's the kids' ashes, not dandruff!

PHIL: Aw, fuck!

> PHIL *maniacally brushes out his hair and his t-shirt. But the shirt gets rubbed in with the ash and dirty.* TANIA *points at various spots in the air.*

TANIA: There's Tony, and David, and Bylinda, and Rachel, and Emily…

> *She giggles.*

SALLY: Fuck! That's disgusting!

> SALLY *shakes out her blanket and hides underneath it.* PHIL *is still brushing himself out.*

TANIA: Hey, Phil, you always wanted to get close to the people.

PHIL: Fuck off. It's getting on you, too.

TANIA: [*realising*] Oh, shit! They're getting in my hair. [*She starts brushing herself over maniacally, too.*] Fuck.

> *She is only managing, like* PHIL, *to rub it into her clothes. The black ashes stop falling.* PHIL *stops trying.*

PHIL: Wind's changing.

> SALLY *looks out from under her blanket and laughs at them both.*

TANIA: Which little shits have I got all over me?

PHIL: Do you reckon it's from one body or bits from several?

TANIA: Don't ask.

PHIL: Sal, will you fucking stop laughing?

> SALLY *laughs harder and hides under her blanket.* PHIL *glares at her and reaches down into the plastic bag. He starts eating.* SALLY *hears the eating and emerges.*

SALLY: Hey, that's for me! That's mine!

PHIL: Can't you see I've got problems of my own?

> TANIA *throws her bag at* SALLY.

TANIA: There you go, then, you needy bitch.

◆ ◆ ◆ ◆ ◆

SEVENTH

Another day.

SALLY *is wrapped up in her blanket, sitting near the trunk.*

PHIL *and* TANIA *enter, carrying school books and pencil cases. They swap notes and begin using highlighters.*

SALLY: Did you bring any food?

> PHIL *shakes his head.*

The school's closed.

TANIA: Derr.

PHIL: Exams are on.

SALLY: What's the point?

PHIL: There's a point to everything.

TANIA: Lie of Success, Number Two.

PHIL: Everything happens for a reason.

> TANIA *and* PHIL *shake their heads and go back to highlighting.*

SALLY: Why can't you study for your stupid exams at home?

PHIL: Dad's a fucking mess. 'Our future, our future.' Have more kids, I tell him. He's got nothing to do, so he just hangs around me asking me stupid non-exam questions, sucking in air.

TANIA: And I'm out in the bungalow now.

SALLY: Sounds like paradise.

TANIA: With my sisters.

PHIL: Those molls. Can't believe your dad put you out there.

TANIA: That whole precautions crap. You know, Dad's smallgoods business. They don't even look at us. They just leave food at the back door. Leaving food at—

She stops and looks at SALLY *who is staring hard now at her.*

Or they…

Pause. SALLY *looks downcast.*

PHIL: [*laughing*] Hey, why don't you let Sally stay with you?

TANIA: [*laughing*] Yeah, right.

PHIL: Serious.

TANIA: Get real. Four girls in a tiny bungalow.

TANIA *laughs.* SALLY *is silent.*

SALLY: I thought I heard a mob come by last night. I hid.

TANIA: Sally could stay in your house.

PHIL: Oh, yeah. And what happens when he lets in all the kids who've been kicked out? What then? He's a teacher. Not a social worker. Makes more sense for Sally to stay with you.

TANIA: Why?

SALLY: You're all girls. It makes sense.

TANIA: But not a stranger. Only family.

SALLY: I'm not a stranger.

Pause. SALLY *begins to laugh at the other two.* TANIA *ignores her and goes back to note-taking and underlining from* PHIL*'s notes.*

You know you're not going to be allowed to do your exams anywhere.

PHIL: Crap.

SALLY *laughs harder. Wrapped in her blanket, she starts crawling around the ground.*

[*To* TANIA] Tan, why are you always working off my notes? Why can't you give me any good notes of yours?

TANIA: Oh, Phil. You take wonderful notes.

SALLY *finds the rotten apple that* PHIL *left near the tree days ago. She has her back to the other two.*

PHIL: But I need to fill the gaps. Yours covers the stuff I cover, but in less detail.

TANIA: Phil. I won't forget you for letting me use your notes.

SALLY *starts eating the old apple.*

PHIL: That's not the point.

SALLY *lets out a moan, a big satisfied moan, now that she finally has found something to eat. She can't help but make noises eating the thing.*

Sal, what the fuck?

He stands up and walks over to her.

Oh, that's fucking disgusting.

TANIA: What's she doing?

PHIL: She's eating that wormy apple.

TANIA: You fucking maggot.

PHIL *dry-retches.* TANIA *runs over and grabs* SALLY*'s blanket.* SALLY *keeps eating the apple.*

Get away from here!

She throws the blanket back at SALLY.

You scab!

PHIL *dry-retches again.* SALLY *is moaning, sort of satisfied.*

You're going to die if I don't kick you myself, you fucking animal!

She runs at SALLY *to kick her.* SALLY *realises and grabs her blanket and runs away.* TANIA *looks at* PHIL *and starts laughing at him.*

Bloody girl. Is that why you hang out with girls? Soon as it gets rough with the boys you want to puke? Faggot.

She laughs at him again.

◆ ◆ ◆ ◆ ◆

EIGHTH

Moonlit night again. PHIL *stands in the darkness. He is sobbing.*

A torchlight comes to rest upon his face. He squints and raises his hands up to it. He puts his arms in the air.

PHIL: I'm sorry.

Silence.

This used to be my land. This is my spot.

Silence.

I like it here.

Silence.

I'll go. I promise I won't come back. I'll go, I'll go!

TANIA: Then piss off, ya bastard.

TANIA *laughs.*

PHIL: Tania? Tania?

TANIA: I just heard.

PHIL: You heard?

TANIA: Damien Harris, the first of the Year Twelves.

PHIL: Maybe we're not immune.

TANIA: No, we are.

PHIL: He came second to me in the practice exams.

TANIA: I know.

PHIL: He wanted to go to Melbourne too.

TANIA: But he wanted to come back. I heard him say.

PHIL: Really?

TANIA: Phil, he wanted to be a vet.

PHIL: So?

TANIA: He didn't really have any ambition.

PHIL: He was one of us.

TANIA: Then why did I choose you and not him?

PHIL: You chose me. [*Beat.*] But... but if Damien can get...

TANIA: Phil, he wanted to be a vet. A country vet. This is where he wanted to stay.

PHIL: Jesus, Sally will—

TANIA: She's a sick bitch already. You saw.

PHIL: Jesus. Damien Harris. What if I'm—?

TANIA: We're going to get the marks and get out. That's our goal.

She moves up to him. She strokes him.

I knew you'd react. That's why I came.

PHIL: You knew?

TANIA: The Lie of Success, Phil. Think of that.

PHIL: What reason?

TANIA: You have one less rival for a university place.

PHIL: Yes. Yes. You're right.

TANIA: That's one less competitor you have to worry about.

PHIL: Yes. Maybe more will get it.

TANIA: We'll be fine.

PHIL: Gee. Maybe this thing will spread to Sandcastle, and keep going down the highway.

TANIA: Only people like us will be left.

PHIL: People who know what needs to be done.

> TANIA *pushes her hand down the front of* PHIL*'s pants.*

TANIA: You don't need to worry about your enemies.

> *She begins to wank him.*

PHIL: The right people will get theirs.

TANIA: Yes.

> PHIL *takes her hand out of his pants.*

PHIL: You'll get my notes back.

> *He guides her hand back in.*

TANIA: Thank you.

> *She starts wanking him again. She whispers nothings to him.*

You're so fucking smart and brave and ambitious.

PHIL: Tell me about other places.

TANIA: I chose you, not Harris.

PHIL: Places.

TANIA: We're the evolved ones. We're the ones who can weather this.

PHIL: Yes.

TANIA: On our own.

> PHIL *frowns and stops her.*

PHIL: I can do it myself.

> *He finishes wanking himself off.* TANIA *tries to kiss him as he is finishing. With his spare hand he tries to push her face away.*

TANIA: You.

> *She grabs the free hand that is pushing her away and starts to kiss him again. He is getting excited by it. He responds. He comes. He is panting, looking ashamed. He looks at her.*

PHIL: This is all disgusting.

TANIA: Yeah.

PHIL: You're disgusting.

> *She laughs at him.*

TANIA: You're still standing.

◆ ◆ ◆ ◆ ◆

NINTH

At the tree.

PHIL *and* TANIA *are surrounded by their notes, textbooks and a pencil case each. They are studying with pens or highlighters at the ready.*

PHIL: You know, this was when swot-vac was meant to be happening.

TANIA: Yes.

PHIL: But our swot-vac started early. That's how I'm re-framing it.

> SALLY *enters. She shuffles up to them. She coughs. The other two ignore her.*

TANIA: Economics. I need to—

PHIL: You want—

TANIA: Correct. I want to re-focus and re-frame so that it's interesting. It's still muck in my head.

PHIL: You want to refocus your inhibiting beliefs.

TANIA: Yes.

SALLY: [*laughing*] You can't do it because you're a slut.

TANIA: Did you hear something?

PHIL: Yeah. I did.

> *He stands up. He walks up to* SALLY *to confront her. She coughs.*

TANIA: Didn't anyone teach you to cover your mouth, you dirty slag?

SALLY: Fuck you. [*She turns her attention to* PHIL.] Phil. Who did you like at school?

PHIL: Dunno.

SALLY: They can be dead or alive.

TANIA: Fuck off, bitch.

SALLY: I know who I liked. Tania knows. [*Beat.*] I've been sleeping when I walk. Have you seen me down the street with the others? Maybe.

We don't talk. I just dream, you know. I am the same age, but it is ten years ago, and when I walk past the closed-down shops, I look in their windows and all that gets reflected is a great big tumour.

PHIL: That's sick.

SALLY: All pus and fat.

She starts coughing again. She can't stop. She is doubling over.

TANIA: She's diseased.

PHIL *says nothing.*

Fuck off, disease!

PHIL: We're meant to be studying.

SALLY: Hey, Tania. Get a load of this.

SALLY *lifts up her shirt. There's a rash on her body.*

TANIA: She's as good as dead. Get away.

TANIA *runs away and exits.*

SALLY: What are you going to do?

She coughs again. PHIL *stands watching. A beat. He makes a fist, raises it, and makes a sudden movement towards her as if he is going to strike. She runs in fear and exits.*

PHIL *looks at his fist from a few different angles, then sits back amongst the textbooks. He makes to keep studying. The wind changes. Black ashes fall from the sky. It takes a moment for him to realise. He flicks at the page. Then he realises. He shouts to the sky.*

PHIL: You stupid dead fucks!

◆ ◆ ◆ ◆ ◆

From here on, whenever the adult characters appear they wear a form of protection, whether it be a breathing mask or white plastic paint protective suit or worse. It depends, of course, on the character, but most of the adult characters act quite loosely with the requirements to keep the protection on.

◆ ◆ ◆ ◆ ◆

TENTH

At the school. MR WORBOYS *holds a protective mask in one hand and a cigarette in the other. He is outside, against a wall having a smoke.*

TANIA *enters.* WORBOYS *jumps back.*

WORBOYS: Christ!

> *He quickly pops his breathing mask to his face. He takes it away a little when he speaks.*

Tania, what the hell are you doing here?

TANIA: Exams are soon.

WORBOYS: There are signs out the front. No unauthorised access.

TANIA: What's unauthorised about me? Schools are for students. I've got a question about money supply and its definitions, Mr Worboys.

WORBOYS: I'm too pissed to deal with you, Tania.

TANIA: I know that there are six levels of money supply, from M-1 to M-6. Which is M-1 again?

WORBOYS: Ask your mate Phil, if he hasn't been chucked on a burning heap.

TANIA: I need to know the definition of M-1 for the exam, to demonstrate my knowledge. Where is the exam going to be?

WORBOYS: Go away, Tania. I'm going to have to report you if you don't.

> *He throws his smoke to the ground and stomps it out. He backs away and exits hurriedly.*

◆ ◆ ◆ ◆ ◆

At the tree. TANIA *meets* PHIL.

TANIA: No luck. Worboys wouldn't give me the date.

PHIL: Remember what MindPower says. Luck is made, not a random event.

TANIA: That's right. We make luck.

PHIL: Why did you see Worboys?

TANIA: I found him.

PHIL: Worboys is a cock. He's not admin. We have to see admin people.

TANIA: Your turn then.

PHIL: I'll do a better job than you.

TANIA: Sure.

PHIL *glares at her.*

PHIL: Do you want to swap some notes?

TANIA: You'll do a better job than me.

She kisses him on the cheek.

◆ ◆ ◆ ◆ ◆

At the school. The office of VICE PRINCIPAL LAWRENCE. *She wears something like a beekeeper's headgear.*

PHIL *enters.*

PHIL: I can't get into Mr Graham's office.

LAWRENCE: He's not here.

PHIL: The school's still functioning without a Principal?

LAWRENCE: How did you get in?

PHIL: The front door was open.

LAWRENCE: Phil, our Principal was one of the lucky adults outside the zone when it got quarantined. If he comes back in, he won't get out for months.

PHIL: Months? Are they talking months? You can take off that stupid mask, Ms Lawrence. I'm not sick. I don't have a rash. No aches or pains. You must be the Acting Principal if he's not here.

LAWRENCE: Correct.

PHIL: You can tell me where the exams are going to be.

LAWRENCE: Phil, the school has not been teaching children since this began. We can hardly send you lot into battle at the exam front. Besides, the papers would not get back to the Board of Studies.

PHIL: What about the Internet?

LAWRENCE: No facilities for that anywhere, Phil. Has to be real paper.

PHIL: This is fucked. We're tougher than the rest. We're alive. We're the real deal. And you won't even let us sit the exams.

LAWRENCE: Phil, you can see the circumstances for yourself.

PHIL: Why don't you do something about the circumstances? You're in the position, now.

LAWRENCE: Next year. If anything opens, you can do your Year Twelve at the TAFE.

41

PHIL: At the TAFE?! A whole year down the drain?!

LAWRENCE: I doubt this school will be given the facilities to meet your needs next year, given the likely enrolments.

PHIL: What?! What about meeting my needs this year?

LAWRENCE: Get real, you drongo. You'll probably die. Forget your fucking exams.

PHIL: I am not going to die.

LAWRENCE: How ironic. None of you little shits wanted to learn when you were alive, and now you lot are kicking the bucket, I get a student who *wants* to do exams.

PHIL: Hold the exams. Hold the fucking exams!

LAWRENCE: Not my call. Nothing I can do.

PHIL: Bullshit.

WORBOYS *enters, mask on.*

WORBOYS: Anne—I heard shouting.

PHIL: [*to* WORBOYS] Drunk arsehole.

WORBOYS: Get out of here!

PHIL *runs out.*

LAWRENCE: That was weird.

WORBOYS: You're telling me. I had another one today, this morning.

LAWRENCE: Why didn't you tell me?

WORBOYS: The paperwork.

LAWRENCE: Who?

WORBOYS: A girl in the same Year Twelve class as him.

LAWRENCE: What did she want?

WORBOYS: When the exams are happening. I laughed at her.

LAWRENCE: Why wouldn't you?

WORBOYS: That's what I asked myself.

LAWRENCE: We'll have to report it.

WORBOYS: And he called me a cunt.

LAWRENCE: Is that what he called you?

WORBOYS: Think so. Irrational, grasping and desperate behaviour. No respect for boundaries. You're right. I should have informed you.

LAWRENCE: I can barely breathe in this thing.

◆ ◆ ◆ ◆ ◆

ELEVENTH

At the tree. TANIA *is studying with* PHIL.

TANIA: I'm not getting any of this.
PHIL: Economics?
TANIA: Talk to me.
PHIL: Why?
TANIA: You're good at explaining things.
PHIL: Don't want to talk. Want to get good marks.

> TANIA *bows her head.*

What are we going to do if she comes back?
TANIA: Punch her out.

> *She crawls over to him and pushes him down on the ground.*

PHIL: What do you want?

> *She unzips his fly.*

TANIA: I just need the right neuro-associative connectors.
PHIL: What?
TANIA: MindPower.
PHIL: I haven't listened to every tape, yet.
TANIA: I need ways of aligning economic theory with what I like.
PHIL: Then do want you like.

> TANIA *stands up and takes her underpants down. She sits down on him.*

What's the problem?
TANIA: Let's start with resource allocation.
PHIL: Are you that far behind?

> *She moves her hips. He groans.*

TANIA: Now.
PHIL: I suppose it is the foundation of our understanding.
TANIA: Good.

> *She starts grinding him.*

PHIL: The basic economic problem is unlimited wants minus limited resources. Those resources consist of four things: land, capital, human and entrepreneurial.

TANIA: That's good. Mh.

PHIL: In the market system we find the most efficient way of allocating those resources to those unlimited wants, filtering out the most extreme of desires, through what Adam Smith defined as the 'invisible hand' operating through the price mechanism.

TANIA: Yes.

She starts getting more excited and frantic.

PHIL: The price mechanism is the signal by which operators in the market know how much resources to allocate to which want. Price is determined by the laws of supply and demand. In the market, people ask for their wants to be met by spending their 'dollar-votes' on the things they need. If demand outstrips supply, the price rises, thus flagging to producers that resources ought to be allocated to that market.

She comes.

TANIA: Oh, God.

PHIL: Am I still a virgin?

TANIA: What?

PHIL: I didn't come.

TANIA: Did I get everything I need for the exam?

PHIL: What else are you having trouble with?

TANIA: Non-accelerating inflation rate of unemployment.

PHIL: Ah, NAIRU.

TANIA: What?

PHIL: It's the acronym. You put it in brackets in the definition in the introduction.

TANIA: What?

PHIL: The capital letters.

TANIA: How does it work?

PHIL: I'm sure I'm still a virgin. Technically.

TANIA: Okay.

She starts fucking him again.

PHIL: The non-accelerating inflation rate of unemployment is a concept which, based on the Phillips curve, indicates that certain low rates of unemployment may drive inflation up beyond a point of no return. That is, when the inflation rate returns to a safer level, that is, price stability returns, the nature of the trade-off between unemployment and inflation has changed, so that only a higher level of unemployment maintains the chief goal of price stability.

She comes.

That was quick.

TANIA: What about you?

PHIL: No cigar.

TANIA: More.

PHIL: Get off me.

TANIA: More.

She finds a rhythm and keeps fucking him.

PHIL: In the Third Republic, galvanised by the leadership of Gambetta, the liberal republic cemented bourgeois democracy through a series of pragmatic deals and compromises with constitutional monarchists. Gambetta believed that politics was the art of the possible—

She stops.

TANIA: What's this?

PHIL: Late nineteenth-century French history.

TANIA: I need economics.

PHIL: It was all I had left in me—why give out gold when I'm not getting any?

TANIA: Fucking prick.

She moves off him violently and then knees him in the balls. He quickly pulls his trousers back up.

You didn't even get us a place to do our exams, you fuck knuckle.

She kicks him.

PHIL: Don't kill the golden goose.

TANIA: What eggs are you laying? Are you shitting golden nuggets? Gambetta? What the fuck has Gambetta got to do with anything?

He gets up gingerly.

PHIL: Do you still have a student number?

TANIA: What's the point? If we can't do our exams, we don't need student numbers, and I don't fucking need you.

PHIL: If we get past the guarded perimeter, all we'll need is a student number.

TANIA: What?

PHIL: If we get to Sandcastle.

TANIA: Dad's panel van.

PHIL: You can drive it?

TANIA: It's an automatic. I can drive an automatic.

PHIL: They always have a few spare exam papers at every exam venue. All we will need is our student numbers. That's all we will need. That and our fake IDs.

TANIA: I'm so sorry.

PHIL: Sure you are.

TANIA: I'm sorry. Forgive me.

> *She gets on her knees, crawls up to him, takes his hand and kisses it.*

PHIL: Let me think.

> *A petal falls.*

◆ ◆ ◆ ◆ ◆

TWELFTH

JOHN *and* GAYLE MOSS *at home. Distantly, the sound of a window pane breakage can be heard.* JOHN *looks out.*

JOHN: Crowd's at number eleven, now. [*Laughing*] Think I see the Deputy Mayor's wife. Good for her.

GAYLE: I don't understand it. John, are you saying that it's all right to terrorise people who are dying?

JOHN: Don't judge people, Gayle.

GAYLE: So what am I allowed to do?

JOHN: They're sending the bulldozers in on the primary school tomorrow. What do you think I want to do?

GAYLE: The point is, you're not doing it.

JOHN: Are you speaking like this outside the house?

GAYLE: Since when do I go outside?

JOHN: We're going to need favours.

GAYLE: Have they fixed up what they're doing with your salary yet?

JOHN: Who knows what the Ministry is doing up there. Everything's in a panic.

46

Beat.

GAYLE: We have to escape.

JOHN: Obviously.

GAYLE: I'm serious.

Pause.

JOHN: As soon as Phil dies we find a way out.

GAYLE: Phil's not sick.

JOHN: He's different.

GAYLE: He's not sick.

JOHN: It might be dormant in him.

GAYLE: He's our boy. He's a good boy. [*Pause.*] He was.

JOHN: Yes.

GAYLE: Used to be… thoughtful.

JOHN: Let's not—

GAYLE: He used to be.

JOHN: Yes. [*Pause.*] I'll call in favours from outside. I still know people in the city who'll be able to help.

Silence. GAYLE *cries.* JOHN *goes down on his knees to her.*

We'll adopt. Foster first, then adopt. Or sponsor.

GAYLE: Yes.

JOHN: I can't wait, can you?

GAYLE: No.

JOHN: Let's celebrate. Before he comes home. Bottle of the champers?

GAYLE *looks at him.*

Every problem is just an opportunity. A challenge. We'll win. We'll get out. You'll see.

❖ ❖ ❖ ❖ ❖

THIRTEENTH

Follows straight on from the eleventh scene.

PHIL *pushes* TANIA *onto the ground on her back and pulls his trousers back down.*

PHIL: Still wet?

TANIA: Define M-1.

He starts fucking her. SALLY *enters the area, silently, dizzily.*

PHIL: M-1 is all cash, bank notes, bond deposits and—

SALLY: You sick fucks.

PHIL *freezes.*

TANIA: More, Phil. More.

SALLY *staggers up to them.*

SALLY: I've spent the day pushing grannies over for their shopping, so don't think I won't bash youse.

PHIL: Jealous, Sal?

SALLY: Fucking bastards.

PHIL: Why be jealous? Your step-daddy fucked you, so what are you afraid of missing out on before you die?

SALLY *lunges at the couple. Both of them jump up and away, getting decent.* TANIA *runs to the tree trunk.*

SALLY: You're a sick cunt.

PHIL *opens his arms out to point at* SALLY.

PHIL: You've got a rash on yours.

TANIA: [*in an excited whisper*] The basic economic problem is unlimited wants versus limited resources.

SALLY: What's she on?

PHIL: That's it, Tan.

TANIA: Those resources consist of four things: land, capital, human and…

PHIL: Come on, Tan!

TANIA: … entrepreneurial!

SALLY *laughs. She backs away from* TANIA. *She points beyond the area.*

SALLY: I can see pyres two and three. Burning away. Might meet you there.

SALLY, *who dumped a bag near the tree, goes to the bag.*

PHIL: Sal, now I associate that image with this empowering place.

SALLY: What do you think I associate it with now?

She pulls out a tent kit.

Luxury.

TANIA: What do you think you're doing?

SALLY: Pitching.

TANIA: Where'd you get that?

SALLY: Some other kid had to die first, didn't she?

PHIL: You're not going to meet us in any pyre, Sal. We're immune. We're getting results.

SALLY: Don't mind me then.

PHIL: We turned this place into an empowering resource for learning.

> PHIL *makes a fist and starts to stride over to* SALLY *to punch her.* TANIA *restrains him.*

TANIA: She'll get hers. It's not worth it.

PHIL: You reckon, do you?

> *He breaks free of* TANIA, *goes to* SALLY*'s tent and begins to pull it up.*

This is my place! You get out of here! This is mine! I've made it!

SALLY: Fuck!

> PHIL *throws bits and pieces all over the place.*

PHIL: You have to understand!

> SALLY *cowers away from him. She starts to run.*

SALLY: You'll get yours!

> *A petal falls from the tree.*

TANIA: Phil…

> *He turns around. They both notice the petal and watch it fall to the ground.* PHIL *looks back up at* TANIA. *He smiles and clicks his tongue.*

PHIL: The drought was life, Tan. Now it's raining, my friend, it's raining.

◆ ◆ ◆ ◆ ◆

FOURTEENTH

A conference room. Five empty, light and uncomfortable seats.

PHIL *and* TANIA *excitedly enter the space and sit next to each other, with big smiles.*

PHIL: They're going to give us our chance.

TANIA: You just have to believe.

MARG BENNETT *enters calmly, smiles at them and sits down.* PHIL *and* TANIA *beam back at her.*

MARG: My name is—please call me Marg.

> PHIL *smiles at* MARG *again.* MARG *looks uncomfortable.*

The others are late.

PHIL: Tardiness.

MARG: [*to* PHIL] Pardon?

PHIL: Tardy. Tardiness. Another word for late. I've been incorporating as many new words as possible into my vocabulary since the start of last year.

TANIA: Sorry, how many more people are coming to see us?

MARG: Just the two.

PHIL: Are they from Melbourne?

MARG: You'd like them to be from Melbourne.

PHIL: It would please me, that's for sure.

MARG: And, Tania, it would please you.

TANIA: Yes.

MARG: And why would that be?

PHIL: You'd be taking our aspirations seriously. I'm sorry. You *are* taking our aspirations seriously.

TANIA: Thanks for making the trip down.

MARG: Do you think I am from Melbourne?

TANIA: Aren't you?

MARG: Originally.

PHIL: You're representing Melbourne, then.

MARG: I replaced two of the other workers in the health centre six months ago, when the centre had to…

PHIL: Restructure.

MARG: Yes.

TANIA: Are you from the Board of Studies or not?

MARG: Would you like me to be?

PHIL: I would like you to be an active proxy with some agency.

MARG: For the moment, it might be better if we all just relax, take a deep breath, and wait for the other two to arrive.

PHIL: Are they from the Board of Studies?

MARG: Would you like them to be?

TANIA: Why do you keep asking us questions like that?

MARG: What would you like me to be doing?

TANIA: I don't know. What's your job?

MARG: What do you think it is?

TANIA: You work for the health centre.

MARG: Asking questions like the ones I am asking you is a core responsibility of my job. To both elicit information and get you to hear the way you present it.

TANIA: You're a social worker. What are you going to do to us?

PHIL: Represent us?

> DR FRANZ *enters.*

FRANZ: Hello, Phil. Hello, Tania. Ms Bennett.

MARG: Marg.

FRANZ: Fine.

> SALLY *enters slowly, unsure of her feet. She looks a mess.*

I believe you already know who this is.

TANIA: What's she doing here?

> PHIL *and* TANIA *glare at* SALLY.

PHIL: Why have we been taken away from our swot-vac to meet up with this thing?

FRANZ: You can sit, Sally.

TANIA: What's going on?

FRANZ: Ms Bennett is in on this session at the Authority's request. Now, it comes to our attention that the three of you associate beyond a certain stage one perimeter restriction. It is very dangerous with this Syndrome to go out at all, let alone beyond that restriction, so close to the hazardous medical waste incineration site.

PHIL: The pyre farm.

FRANZ: Let's keep a cool head, if we can, Phil.

PHIL: Everybody calls it that.

TANIA: [*at* SALLY] You slut.

> SALLY *smiles back at* TANIA.

MARG: It's all right, Sally.

FRANZ: Phil, Tania, we have also had reports to the Authority that you—

MARG: [*to* PHIL *and* TANIA] Young bodies and minds, under stress in times like these, might partake in behaviours which in the long run lead to even more stress—

PHIL: There'll be no long run at this rate—

FRANZ: —and who knows how reproductive hormones could agitate the—

MARG: And it's perfectly understand(able)—

FRANZ: Quite frankly, the behaviour which has been witnessed by at least three independent witnesses is abnormal. Both Ms Bennett and I have made assessments of this evidence to the Authority, and we just have to ensure that you are of no further danger to the community. These abnormal characteristics have led us to believe, given the progression of the Syndrome as I have witnessed it, that you may be habouring possible mutations of whatever disease, virus or bacteria that may be leading to the Hollow Syndrome.

PHIL: Utter bullshit. Give me someone from the Authority.

TANIA: [to SALLY] You fucking little diseased slut.

FRANZ: I am the representative for the Authority.

PHIL: You cannot seriously believe, that without a rash, a cough, we have this… this thing that she's got. Give us someone from Melbourne.

MARG: If we did, how would that make you feel?

TANIA: [to MARG] Why don't you shut up? You're a fucking slag bitch, too.

PHIL: I could put my case. They'd listen to my case and I'd persuade them!

TANIA: I'm not sick. Look!

> TANIA *starts jumping and bouncing around.*

SALLY: Good one, you moll.

PHIL: How the fuck do you think it would make me feel? [*To* FRANZ] What's she doing here anyway?

MARG: At the Authority's request, I provide a social perspective on the pathologies Dr Franz must deal with.

TANIA: See—I'm not sick.

> *She grabs her seat and moves to attack* SALLY *with it.*

Ya fucking moll!

PHIL: Don't! We've still got a chance!

> *He restrains* TANIA.

FRANZ: This mutation obviously prolongs the host. Maybe it is bacterial. While the physical symptoms are dormant, you should both be doing nothing—

> SALLY *laughs at* TANIA.

—Nothing to provoke the onset of the syndrome.

> TANIA *puts the chair down for a moment; she continues to glare at* SALLY.

Engage in as little mental, emotional—and from what I hear—sexual stimulation as possible.

TANIA: [*overlapping, frantically whispering*] The non-accelerating inflation rate of unemployment is a concept which, based on the Phillips curve / [*continuing under the others' speeches*] indicates that certain low rates of unemployment may drive inflation up beyond a point of no return. That is, when the inflation rate returns to a safer level, that is, price stability returns, the nature of the trade-off between unemployment and inflation has changed, so that only a higher level of unemployment maintains the chief goal of price stability—

SALLY: See? She's going crazy. She was having sex saying these things.

FRANZ: In this state, you will only provoke what is already there to flare physically. No learning or study. It could kill you, or pose an even greater public health risk. Tania, we should make a uterine examination immediately—

SALLY: Phil [*mock weeping*] —it's too late for Tania. And it's too late for me. Maybe it's not too late for you. So listen to them, mate. They want what's best for us. I know you've had itches, and Tania says she wants kids, but—

> MARG *moves over to* SALLY *and puts her arms around her shoulders.*

PHIL: Bullshit!

SALLY: Listen to them, mate. Please.

PHIL: Lying, diseased hick!

FRANZ: Contain yourselves!

PHIL: Right. Right. Contain myself. Right.

> TANIA *finishes her speech.*

Right. [*Nodding*] Contain myself. I'll contain myself all right. Bring the exam papers to town. Put me in a protective suit. I'll sit in a vacuum chamber with an oxygen mask and fucking write my essay in rubber gloves. What else do I have to prove to you?

MARG: Sally, does Phil normally act this way?

> SALLY *shakes her head.*

TANIA: Cunts! Cunts!

TANIA *hurls the chair at them.* PHIL *kicks over chairs as well. They begin trashing everything, yelling.* MARG *hurdles* SALLY *into a corner and protects her.* DR FRANZ *runs out when* PHIL *rushes them.*

FRANZ: [*calling out*] Sedatives! Sedatives!

PHIL *and* TANIA *look at each other; angrily.*

PHIL: You've fucked up everything!

TANIA: You have!

They look at the huddled two.

Not worth it.

TANIA *spits at them.*

PHIL: Come on!

PHIL *and* TANIA *exit, running. Pause.*

MARG: Are you all right, Sally?

SALLY: That was fun.

MARG: How are you feeling?

SALLY: Great.

MARG: I have to say, Dr Franz seems to be a little provocative. He makes all the pronouncements. I don't get a look in.

SALLY: That's because he's a cunt.

MARG: You're a fighter, aren't you?

SALLY: I live.

MARG: Sally. Can I ask you a favour?

SALLY: A favour.

MARG: I'm going to ask you to trust me.

SALLY *giggles.*

Yes. That sounds good. [*Beat.*] You haven't yet reached the final stages of the Syndrome.

SALLY: Yeah. Kidneys and liver haven't sent the attack cells to the brain yet. Lungs aren't gasping.

MARG: How terrible. You've seen it.

SALLY: How many kids have been kicked out?

SALLY *takes a big gulp of air and holds it.*

MARG: What are you doing?

Silence.

Sally! No!

SALLY: Just impersonating.

> SALLY *laughs.*

MARG: Sally. You're going to have to trust me.

SALLY: Why?

MARG: This, I believe, is one of the truly postmodern diseases. A new type of disease for the third millennium. I am writing an article for a journal putting this view. I want to research you, if you will let me, before the final stages. I want to look at the social dimensions of the Syndrome.

> SALLY *yawns.*

You would be my major case study.

> SALLY *yawns again, loudly.*

It would be one way you could live on.

> *Pause.*

SALLY: What's in it for me?

> *Beat.*

MARG: Well—

> SALLY *punches* MARG *in the body. She punches her again and again, until* MARG *is on the floor in agony.*

SALLY: Your wallet!

> MARG *produces her wallet for* SALLY. SALLY *grabs it. She straightens up and loses her footing momentarily. She kicks* MARG, *then takes a big breath, and like an exhausted runner, gets out of the conference room.*

◆ ◆ ◆ ◆ ◆

FIFTEENTH

At the tree.

PHIL *is digging with a shovel. He makes a small hole. He strikes metal.*

PHIL: [*muttering*] More shallow than…

> *He peers into it.* TANIA *arrives.*

55

TANIA: I've got the car. What's that?

PHIL: A shovel.

TANIA: What did you do with it?

PHIL: Wouldn't you like to know? Recreation. Been waiting.

TANIA: Haven't got much to go with.

PHIL: What? Haven't you got the car?

TANIA: That's all fine. Got the petrol.

PHIL: But?

TANIA: Did you get any food?

PHIL: Nup. Just grabbed my pencil case, and ID. You were bringing the food.

TANIA: They hardly left any. Think my sisters have been selling it.

PHIL: Isn't one of them going down?

TANIA: Yeah. Show me your ID. Is it good?

> PHIL *gets out his ID.*

PHIL: It's good.

TANIA: International Student Association. Same as mine.

PHIL: You're twenty-one.

TANIA: And you're twenty. They'll have to let us out.

PHIL: Say that we got lost on a back road visiting a mate.

TANIA: You look too young.

PHIL: For what?

TANIA: For twenty.

PHIL: And you? Twenty-one? At least the photo matches. You're tired.

TANIA: You look fucked.

> *She lifts up his shirt behind him and checks his back.*

You don't have a bloody rash, do you?

PHIL: No! [*Pause.*] Define M-3.

TANIA: M-3 is all cash, with bank deposits and…

PHIL: Come on.

TANIA: … and… something… Fuck!

PHIL: You need me.

TANIA: You need the car.

PHIL: You want to work out what we're doing once we get there. But we have to stay on top of the game, competitive, that way we'll be motivated.

TANIA: I'm going to do better than you are.

PHIL: That's the spirit. You're wrong, but that's the spirit.

TANIA: So what do we do once we're in Sandcastle?

PHIL: How d'you mean?

TANIA: Food. Shelter.

PHIL: Get real—it's a panel van.

TANIA: That's where I'm sleeping.

PHIL: Fuck off then.

TANIA: What about food then?

PHIL: We'll get what we need.

TANIA: We haven't got it.

PHIL: We'll work out something. [*He looks her up and down.*] We'll work out something.

TANIA: I'm so hungry, Phil. I'm so hungry.

PHIL: Believe.

◆ ◆ ◆ ◆ ◆

SIXTEENTH

Follows straight on from the previous scene.

SALLY *enters, walking with something similar to a drunken swagger. She is carrying a crumpled brown paper bag with something in it. She puts in on the ground.*

SALLY: Not giving up, are youse?

> PHIL *and* TANIA *freeze in fright.*

Were you digging up some grub, Phil?

TANIA: Phil—

PHIL: Why don't you get stuffed, you piece of shit?

> *He goes up to her and pushes her over with his foot.*

TANIA: Phil!

PHIL: You made that happen.

TANIA: Come on. Before she dobs us in again.

SALLY: Nice hole, Phil.

PHIL: Yeah, just for you. Serves you right. You wanted to stay here, go on. Be our guest. Stay here in Hollow. We're looking to the future.

TANIA: Come on, Phil.

TANIA *moves to leave for good.*

SALLY: You hungry?

TANIA *stops.*

I'm not hungry anymore. I'm fine. In the paper bag. Brought some milk.

PHIL: Bullshit.

TANIA *runs to the bag and grabs it. She pulls out a container.* PHIL *grabs the other container in the bag.* TANIA *drinks it straight away.* PHIL *sniffs the container.*

You cunt.

SALLY: What?

TANIA *starts choking and gasping.* SALLY *falls about, cackling.*

PHIL: [*to* TANIA] Why didn't you smell it first, you idiot?

TANIA *is gasping and coughing.*

It smelt like Draino. Why did you drink it?

PHIL *chucks the stuff at* SALLY. TANIA *tries to retch.*

Get in the car, Tania. Get in the car. Don't try to vomit. It'll burn your throat on the way up again, you fool. You fool! Get in the car! Fuck. I'll have to drive.

PHIL *bustles* TANIA *away with him. He just remembers to pick up his pencil case and take it with him.* SALLY *keeps on laughing like a little child. She starts picking up petals and watching them drop, laughing when they do. Suddenly she jumps up and stands. She yells at the pile.*

SALLY: You lazy-arsed bludgers! Do I have to do everything?! Serves you right! Serves you right!

She semi-collapses and crawls into the hole that PHIL *dug.*

◆ ◆ ◆ ◆ ◆

Well away from the tree, at the perimeter.

A security guard, JONESY, *walks on and meets* PHIL *who is coming from the opposite direction.*

JONESY: What's wrong with your car, mate. Turn back.

PHIL *nervously smiles and puts on a very broad country accent.*

PHIL: Aw, mate, transmission's stuffed on the old banger, must have strayed into this off me mate's property.

JONESY: What were you doing?

PHIL: Study at the Ag College in Sandcastle, mate. We all do.

JONESY: [*indicating* TANIA, *offstage*] What, she do Ag too?

PHIL: Look, I can understand why you'd want a frigging border around Hollow, the hole.

JONESY: Yeah.

PHIL: Don't you do the bouncing at the Standard?

JONESY: Yeah. We did. But we got contracted for this. Haven't been back home for weeks. Feels like months.

PHIL: Yeah, well it oughta blow over soon, eh mate?

JONESY: See your ID.

PHIL: Sure thing, mate.

> *He produces his ID.*

JONESY: Twenty.

PHIL: Sweet.

JONESY: [*pointing off to* TANIA] I'll need to see hers, too.

PHIL: What?

JONESY: I'll need to see hers.

PHIL: Yeah, understandable. Wouldn't want any mongrel from Hollow getting through, would ya? Bloody awful place these days, by the sound of it.

JONESY: [*calling*] Miss. Forward.

PHIL: She's feeling a bit under the weather, what with the kid and that. Gotta get back to Sandcastle.

JONESY: Get her.

> PHIL *goes offstage and drags* TANIA *in. She is just about doubled over in pain; she looks incredibly unwell. She is carrying two pencil cases.*

TANIA: What? What's going on?

JONESY: ID.

> PHIL *gives her ID to him.*

She twenty-one?

PHIL: [*to* TANIA] Darlin', you lied to me.

He laughs. JONESY *is unmoved.*

JONESY: What part of Sandcastle?

TANIA *stumbles.* PHIL *catches her.*

PHIL: Sorry?

JONESY: You live in Sandcastle. What part?

Silence.

All right, then. Haven't you heard? They've raised the absolute no-readmittance age here.

PHIL: What, mate?

JONESY: They raised it to twenty-two.

PHIL *loses his accent.*

PHIL: What?!

JONESY: Can't let you in. Most fake IDs don't go over twenty-two. Just enough to get you into a pub maybe, but not out of a quarantine.

TANIA: But we've got exams.

PHIL: We have to do our exams. [*Beat.*] We're both fucked if we stay in Hollow.

JONESY *indicates* TANIA *to* PHIL. PHIL *takes a moment and then pushes* TANIA *forward.* JONESY *circles her, slowly undoing his protective suit and reaching inside to undo his fly.* TANIA *is only half-aware and looks about to be violently ill.*

It won't take long, Tan.

TANIA: My… my…

JONESY: What's she saying?

He approaches her and touches her face to hold her head and look in her eyes. TANIA *tries to pull her head away from his grasp.*

Uh, uh.

She vomits over him, into his protective suit.

Oh, fucking cunt of a thing!

PHIL *begins to back away.* JONESY *still hasn't worked out what to do. So* PHIL *runs up to* TANIA. *She looks at him.*

PHIL: [*to* TANIA] You drank it, you fucking idiot.

He grabs the pencil cases from her and exits. JONESY *is slowly beginning to get very angry.*

60

JONESY: Never had to wash it out from the inside… you moll.

TANIA: I feel sick.

JONESY *looks into his suit.*

JONESY: I noticed. [*Calm seems to come over him.*] What did you think you were doing? Getting out? With that story?

TANIA: Exams.

JONESY: Exams? You Hollow people are pretty desperate, aren't you? How old are you, really?

TANIA: Seventeen.

JONESY: Right…

TANIA *is shivering. He looks at her.*

You're sweet, aren't you?

She doesn't answer.

You've got a rash on your neck.

He readjusts his balls and then grabs her shoulder.

Why don't you come and join the other cum-buckets?

TANIA: Phil?

JONESY: Come on.

He grabs her head to examine it closer. He puts his fingers in her mouth and looks inside for defects.

No signs round the mouth. You'll do. For a while.

He grabs her by the ear and begins to haul her away.

This situation fucking rocks.

As he drags her away he whistles.

◆ ◆ ◆ ◆ ◆

SEVENTEENTH

At the tree.

SALLY *is in the hole. You can hear her pant.*

PHIL *returns. He stops and looks up at the tree.*

PHIL: Beautiful sight. Nice landscape. See you. [*He goes up to the hole.*] Come on, Sal. Get out of my hole. It's mine. [*He bends down to talk to her.*] You're still breathing.

Silence.

Come on. Get out of my hole. I dug it. Hey. Do you want to come with me?

SALLY *makes a mumbling sound.* PHIL *bends into the hole and pulls her up. She makes almost baby noises.*

Good. Good. You can still hear me. Sal, you are sitting on top of my hole. You are blocking my hole.

She laughs. He tries to think of ways to get her out. She is too heavy for him.

Can you still walk?

SALLY: Bye-bye.

PHIL: Come on.

He gets into the hole and props her up.

Do you want to hear a bye-bye story?

SALLY: Bye-bye.

PHIL: Good.

SALLY *still has the ability to wrap her arms around him.*

Good-good.

SALLY: Good-good.

PHIL *strains to shift her bodyweight as he talks. As he speaks he succeeds in getting her out of the hole by the last bit of the story.*

PHIL: Here goes. You know most of it. Once upon a time, I used to live on a farm. A stupid, little hobby farm where Mum used to go about planting trees and ignoring Dad—

SALLY: Trees—

PHIL: But one day, before we had to sell up to the dickhead from the city, I stumbled across workmen in a field. I got scared and ran away. The next day they were there again. And I ran away again. But the third day, they had cranes and pipes and bulldozers, and Mum was planting that tree—

SALLY: Tree, tree—

PHIL: Yeah—and so I went up to a workman and asked where the pipes would take me. And the workman laughed and all his mates laughed and he said, well, if you go one way, they'll take you to the ocean.

But, he said, if you go the other and you follow your nose, you'll get to any bathroom in Melbourne you desire.

SALLY *is unresponsive.* PHIL *dumps her. He runs and gets the shovel.*

And I looked at the tree and I measured and memorised the spot.

He prises open a metallic grating with the aid of the shovel's blade. SALLY *walks to the edge of the hole. She dopily peers in. For a moment, the stink sort of seems to wake her up.*

SALLY: Stinks!

PHIL *pushes her away.*

PHIL: It's my hole. I dug it. I own it. I'm getting in. You can choose to rot like the vegetable you are, but I am going to make a difference.

He disappears down the hole. The grating comes down with a thud on top of him. SALLY *laughs. Stops. She stands vacantly again at the grating's edge. She bends down to try to pull at it, but now she has weakened too much for her effort to be of any use. She examines her hands.*

SALLY: Get away from me. [*Looking at her feet.*] Get away from me.

She grunts at each hand, then each foot. She is standing with her legs apart, her hands far from her body. Even though she is standing reasonably still, you can see that she is panicking, her head and eyes twitching from side to side, carefully regarding her own body as if at any moment the legs, the hands, the stomach might attack her head. She breathes hard in this struggle. GAYLE MOSS *enters.*

GAYLE: Oh. Sally.

JOHN MOSS*'s voice can be heard from a distance.*

JOHN: [*offstage*] For fuck's sake, Gayle. What's wrong with you?

GAYLE: Quiet, John.

JOHN MOSS *enters.*

JOHN: Oh.

SALLY *slowly turns her head to them. Her arms are outstretched.*

GAYLE: I thought I saw Phil.

JOHN: You stopped the car for that? Jesus. I am waiting in the car for you. Three minutes. That is all. I can survive without you, you know. Three minutes; that's it.

*He leaves.*SALLY *grunts.*

GAYLE: I planted that tree.

A petal falls from above.

It still grows. Amazing. Beautiful landscape.

SALLY *grunts at* GAYLE.

I don't have anything.

SALLY *grunts again, fearfully. One foots makes a clumsy lunge in* GAYLE's *direction.*

[*Backing away, frightened*] Don't ask me for anything. I told you. [*She steadies herself before leaving. In a harsh whisper*] You kids brought it on yourselves.

GAYLE *exits.* SALLY, *wild-eyed, stands rooted to the spot, panicking at the slightest twitch either of her outstretched arms make. Petals begin to fall around at a very fast and steady rate, almost like water from a waterfall.* SALLY *breathes very hard. Ashes and white dust fall down, too.*

SALLY: No.

She takes one last gasp and holds her breath, eyes bulging. Blackout.

THE END

www.ingramcontent.com/pod-product-compliance
Lightning Source LLC
Chambersburg PA
CBHW041933090426
42744CB00017B/2036